State of Newsgames 2020

A snapshot analysis of interactives, toys and games in
journalism and allied industries

ISBN: 978-1-716-90752-4

Overview

This report provides an overview of the common attributes of current news focused games and interactives. It aims to provide a snapshot of the state of newsgames and related digital media a decade after much of the original work on the topic was produced. It offers observations about the subjects covered, mechanics, aesthetic and experiential qualities of such designed experiences.

This is not meant to be a comprehensive evaluation of ludic news experiences; it is aimed instead to provide a wide topographical view of the landscape of primarily English-language based newsgames and toys produced between 2015 and 2020.

Findings include a relatively limited set of innovations in mechanics for such play and heavy focus on politics, business practices, and empathy. The vast majority of games researched were 2-dimensional games, primarily produced by professional news organizations using HTML5 and JavaScript. Nearly all could be completed in less than 10 minutes and offered only one ostensible level. These news focused experiences predominately employ choose your own adventure or action game mechanics, use a limited color palette, and are most often editorial in nature.

Readers of this report should gain a better understanding of the commonalities of such design. It provides a snapshot of emerging tendencies in the characteristics of newsgames and toys. Much like defining the qualities of a political cartoon, the researchers aim to demonstrate a few aesthetic and experiential characteristics of newsgames and toys.

Authors:

Lindsay Grace

Lindsay is Knight Chair in Interactive Media at the University of Miami School of Communication. He is Vice President for the Higher Education Video Game Alliance and the 2019 recipient of the Games for Change Vanguard award. He authored or co-authored more than 70 papers, articles and book chapters on games since 2009. These include Doing Things with Games, Social Impact through Design (2019 Taylor and Francis) and Love and Electronic Affection: A Design Primer (2020 Taylor and Francis).He has been researching newsgames and persuasive play since 2011.

https://professorgrace.com/

Katy Huang:

Katy is a graduate student and research assistant at the University of Miami School of Communication with a concentration in UX/UI design. With a background in art and advertising, her work has been published on Ads of the world, Graphis and Adstasher.

https://www.katy-huang.com/

Report Citation:
Grace, Lindsay & Haung, Katy. *State of Newsgames 2020.* JournalismGames.com, Miami, Florida, USA. July, 8 2020.

Introduction:

Newsgames are generally defined as playable experiences that focus on current topics, often with the aim of applying some type of journalistic principles to their creation. These might include games that aim to editorialize, report, demonstrate, or explain contemporary news topics. Bogost et al. emphasize a wide definition of news games, offering that they are "a broad body of work produced at the intersection of videogames and journalism" [1]. Others like Gonzalo Frasca emphasize the editorial elements of play [3]. Among them is the perspective that offers newsgames as a kind of "simulation meets political cartoon" championed by Treanor and Mateas [14]. More inclusively, Sicart defines them as "games that "utilize the medium with the intention of participating in the public debate" [13]. More recently researchers like Kluas aim to define it through methodical analysis of practice, identifying boundary work [8].

Ultimately, the theme that ties all of these definitions together is the relationship of the designed play experience to contemporary news items, with an aim to impart with journalistic integrity or informed opinion. For this reason and for clarity in writing, the team has chosen the widely applicable definition of work at the intersection of journalism and game design. From the contemporary practice of newsgame creation between 2015-2020, the term allows for a collection of commonly practiced playful designs including not only conventional arcade games and choose your own adventure games, but also playful quizzes and related content.

The most oft referenced early works in the digital domain of newsgames include September 12th [4] and Darfur is Dying[11]. These stand as great examples of such work, but they also give evidence to a commonly narrow definition of newsgames.

Such examples miss some of the wider array of ludic news focused play. If considering the definitions of newsgames as offered, the digital equivalents of the playful quizzes that once filled the printed back pages of a Cosmopolitan magazine, might also fall into a more inclusive categorization of newsgames. Just as Bogost et al reference the crossword as a part of newsgame history, the quizzes that offered feedback on *what kind of lover you are* or assessed *your dynamic with your friends* can also be considered part of this array.

While ostensibly not about contemporary news, the reality is that many such quizzes were an echo of contemporary politics, transitioning sometimes toward feminism, but often against [9]. Osterman and Keller-Cohen, in particular argue that the "quiz, apparently playful feature in these magazines, is not as harmless as it appears to be" [9]. In the first chapter of Bogost, Ferrari's and Schweizer's Newsgame book, they remind their reader that "games have been a part of the news for almost a century, since the first 'word cross' puzzles appeared in the New York Sunday World in 1913." All such play, whether crossword quiz or love tester, are intertwined with the history of news and audience.

Scholars of newsgames may argue that such ludic quizzes are not in fact games, but another type of interaction. It is therefore more inclusive to describe the research contained in this paper as involving primarily newsgames and news toys. As explained in the diagram to the left, there is an easy way to differentiate designed based on the amount of play supported and the formal play structure. At the base is an interactive, simply any experience that allows a user to act and provides feedback. A toy adds support for play in that interaction, and a game structures the play of a toy into a full fledge game, typically with a win or lose condition [7]. This definition seems to support the ways in which news organizations both flirt with and commit to newsgames as solutions.

When the bulk of digital newsgames research was first published such play was considered new and novel, despite the clear observations that some sorts of news-toys (e.g. quizzes) had existed in digital form. Researchers offered both speculation on potentials and propensities (Bogost, et al.) as well as case studies [16], [12], [15]. Such case study analysis continues [12] alongside some critique of the current state of such work [5].

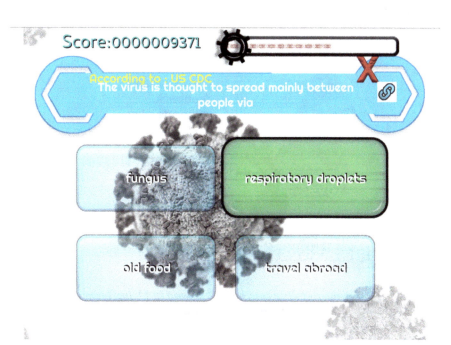

Score:0000009371

According to : US CDC
The virus is thought to spread mainly between people via

fungus

respiratory droplets

old food

travel abroad

This journey is based on extensive research and real stories of Syrians who have made the journey.

Select your character to begin your journey

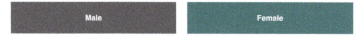

Male

Female

The simple COVID-19 Trivia Quiz and the BBC's Syrian Journey demonstrate the range of news games, from simple playful quizzes to complex choose your own adventure games.

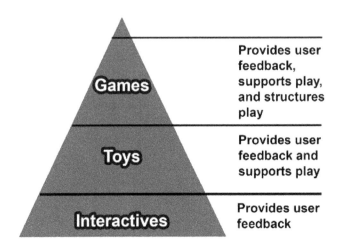

The games, toys and interactives hierarchy as explained in Doing Things with Games: Social Impact through Design [7]

Since its introduction the idea has become less novel and its practice has been undertaken by a wider array of practitioners. It, like many solutions subject to a hype cycle, may have experienced a rise and fall. As Maxwell Foxman puts it in 2015, "after a surfeit of investment in the second half of the 2000s, newsgames lost favor with producers and financiers" [2]. He offers that the source of this decline includes "the paucity of fun newsgames, the insularity of serious newsgame designers within the game design world, and the ubiquity of independent games which could address news subjects but didn't necessarily abide by journalistic principles" [2].

It is clear, that while there was a healthy collection of seminal work on the promise of news games, there is a need to address the issues identified. This research sets out to take a snapshot of the current status of newsgames to help address some of those issues. Namely, by providing a snapshot of the state of newsgames we hope to decrease the insularity of the practice, supporting an increased understanding of what makes newsgames fun or engaging, and how journalism organizations and indie games have addressed abiding by journalist principles.

Instead of aiming to provide a comprehensive view of the practice, this work aims to provide a snapshot of the current state of practice in newsgame design and implementation. It is done so to help both researchers and practitioners understand where the practice has moved since the now decade-old seminal work was first published.

One of the expected benefits of such work is in aiding the community of practitioners in understand what has already been done and how it's been done. For individuals and teams starting such work there are few comprehensive and up to date resources to see the contemporary state of practice. Newsgames are offered, in part, as a subset of collections offered by organizations like the Games for Change game collection (http://www.gamesforchange.org/games/) and other serious games website collections.

The challenges with such resources are many. First, they are often self-selecting. The individuals behind a game choose to submit their work to such organizations for inclusion. This does little to address "the insularity of serious newsgame designers within the game design world" [2]. For this reason, this team of researchers sought newsgame work beyond that which is listed in common clearinghouses and for which game design awards have been given. The aim is not to analyze that which the games community is already familiar, but to expand the games community's awareness of what news organizations have done (and vice-versa).

In compliment, the researchers produced a publicly available website, JournalismGames.org, that allows researchers to view the work from which this research was conducted. This includes the ability to produce their own queries on the same data the researchers collected on newsgames and toys. In the end, the goal is to provide transparency and increase accessibility.

By archiving the games, through image, text and video the researchers aim to support the ability of new practitioners and researchers examining the history of newsgames and considering engaging in their own project. It is hoped such archiving, in both publication and website, will help with addressing insularity. In the least, it is hoped that such work will help designers and developers avoid repeating past mistakes, while moving the practice forward.

Research Methodology

The researchers collected 50 games which rest within the conventional understanding of newsgames or news toys as defined in the introduction. These games were somewhat chosen at random, although the data set excluded games that were created as part of game jams or that failed to have a substantial play record (considered to be 10,000 or more plays as listed publicly). A list of more than 100 such games was paired down to 50 by reviewing news articles describing new releases in the newsgame space and culling case study analysis provided through prior research [2], [6]. Each of these experiences was played to completion, screen captured, and catalogued for this research. The data was collected in a relational database, the contents of which are provided at JournalismGames.org for further analysis by other researchers.

Definitions:

Based on the contemporary state of newsgames and related playable media, it is useful to offer a kind of categorization and definition of the various design aims of such work. While categorizations are often evolving, the following set is heuristic based. Instead of working from a theoretical frame and then seeking to note work that has these elements, these definitions were derived from first examining work and then discern the ways in which they are distinct. It is a set of definitions based on what has been made, less than what could be. Ultimately these categorizations and definitions orbit those offered in the seminal work of Bogost et. al's categorizations[1].

The functional definitions for the type of newsgames, interactives and toys includes:

- **Alternative Reporting**: experiences provided as an alternative means to understanding an accompanying traditional article. Alternative reporting work is typically offered in parallel to an article as a way of experiencing or explaining the content in the article.

- **Documentary**: work designed to provide a journalist documentary of a person, population or event with an aim toward historical record. Such work borrows elements of documentary work in film and related media and may be a self-described docugame or similar effort.

- **Editorial:** ludic work whose journalistic distance and efforts to provide fair and balanced reporting are subsumed by the work's intention to sway the player toward a strongly biased, often critical perspective.

- **Playable Infographic**: visual data toy, game or playable interactive typically meant to convert numerical data sets into ludic visual representations. Such infographics may be classified within the milieux of newsgames when they employ ludic characteristics, such as encouraging users to play with data-based scenarios or experiment with content for dynamic visualizations.

- **Media Literacy**: experiences designed to increase player understanding of news media, typically around understanding information sources as they relate to mis-information and dis-information.

- **Quiz:** Ludic assessments, often derived around understanding self, but sometimes designed to help the player match themselves to some news item (e.g. which kind of Olympic athlete could you be, which political candidate matches your values, etc).

- **Reportage**: designs aiming to report contemporary news through a ludic experience, as opposed to offering a documentary, reportage games convert what would typically have been a journalist experience into a playable experience. Reportage games are often the product of derived from an aggregate set of articles or a news series.

Findings

To capture data about the general experience offered for players, the researchers aimed to describe the designs aim, the topics covered in the experience, and the general game mechanics delivered. Each received a primary and secondary categorization of the work's intention as either media literacy, documentary, reportage, playable infographic, alternative reporting tool, quiz or editorial.

The basic criteria for these categorizations was adapted from Bogost et. al's categorizations, to mean [1]:

- Media Literacy (2 games):
- Documentary (5 games):
- Reportage (3 games):
- Infographic (4 games):
- Alternative Reporting (4 games):
- Quiz (8 games):
- Editorial (24 games)

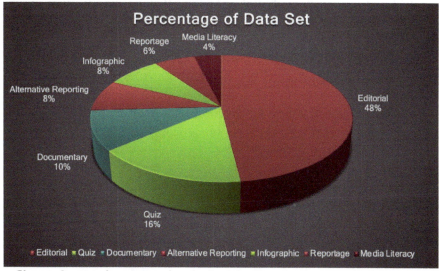

Chart indicating the categorical makeup of the 50-game data set, based on primary categorization.

The games were also categorized for their topical focus. The three most popular topics were politics (24% or 11 games), corporate business practices (14% or 7 games), and games focused on producing empathy for specific populations (14% or 7 games). Other topics included budget management, sports and adventure, all of which accounted for 8% or 4 games each in the set.

Prime examples of political games include:
- Brexit Bus (https://advisa.se/en/research/brexit-bus/)
- Trump's Pussy Grabber (http://pussygrabber.com/)
- Angry Olds (https://everydayarcade.com/games/angry-olds).

Business practice games include:
- Building your own Trading Bot
  (https://www.wsj.com/graphics/build-your-own-trading-bot/)
- You are Jeff Bezos, where would the HQ2 go?
  (https://stories.usatodaynetwork.com/amazon).

Empathy focused games include:
- BBC's Syrian Journey (https://www.bbc.com/news/world-middle-east-32057601)
- The Waiting Game (https://projects.propublica.org/asylum/)

It's also useful to understand the mechanics that are used in such games. The most common in the set was choose your own adventure games at 44%. Examples include:
- Vox Media's College Scholarship Tycoon
  (https://apps.voxmedia.com/graphics/vox-college-admissions-game/)
- Vice's choose your own adventure, Renting
  (https://www.vice.com/en_uk/article/9ke547/choose-your-own-adventure-renting).

The second most common were arcade action experiences at 20%. Examples of such include:
- Every Arcade's Bomb the Right Place
  (https://everydayarcade.com/games/bomb-the-right-place)

The third most common group were quizzes at 6% examples include:
- Could You Be Speaker
  (https://www.thetimes.co.uk/article/could-you-be-speaker-house-of-commons-bercow-xck6lxv98)

Who Makes Newsgames and Toys?

From the dataset, 18 news organizations, 3 financial services institutions, 3 social responsibility non-profits, 2 universities and 2 news game organizations, produced the work. The news organizations included traditional news standards like the New York Times and the Washington Post, new media organizations like Vox and Vice, and largely state monitored sources like the Straights Time in Singapore. Everyday Arcade and Persuasive Games were the most prolific of all.

Given the English language selection, the work was primarily produced by organizations in the USA and UK, although work was also produced in The Netherlands, Singapore, and Brazil. Some games were offered in multiple languages.

Experience

Beyond cataloging the stated aims of each, the researchers noted a variety of experiential characteristics of the games to better understand the shape of such designs. 35, or 70% of the games, could be completed in 5 minutes of less. Eight games , or 16% of the data set could be completed between 5-10 minutes. Figure 2 illustrates the length of play.

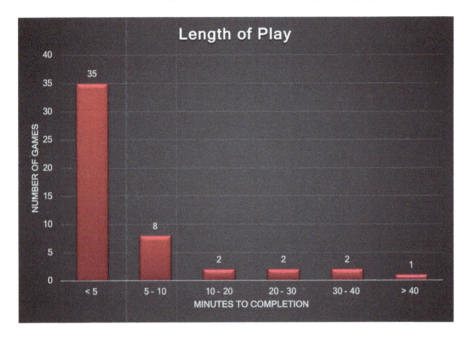

Chart indicating how long each game offered play, measured as length of time between game start and completion.

Exactly 50% of the games, or 25 of them, offered audio and the other half did not. The 90% (or 45) of the experiences were made playable through HTML5 and JavaScript, typically as output through tools like Twine, Construct 3, or other game building tools. The remaining 10 were flash playable games, which also represented the oldest games in the set (dating to 2014 or earlier).

Aesthetics

Understanding the aesthetic patterns of the games helps provide a glimpse into their design. The simplicity of aesthetic representation hints at a variety of characteristics including budget. Aesthetic qualities are some times the product technical constraints, such as game engine support, web browser capabilities and computational complexity. As has been shown in prior analysis of general persuasive play, newsgames are primarily 2D experiences with simple graphical characteristics.

76% of the experiences, or 38 of them, were 2-Dimensional. 12%, or 6 games, used real-life photography or video. 3 games provided no graphics at al., 2 were offered in a locked isometric perspective (similar to 2.5 D), and only 1 game in the data set was 3D.

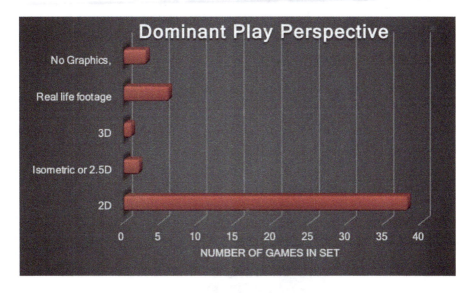

Chart indicating graphical perspective and style of all games in the data set.

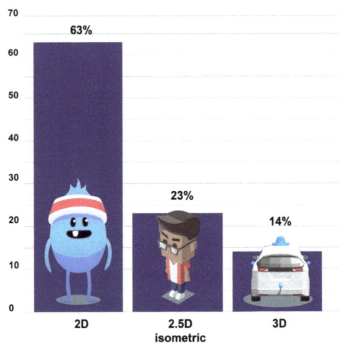

Examples of 2D, 2.5D Isometric and 3D representations in illustrating their percentage distribution in the newsgames studied.

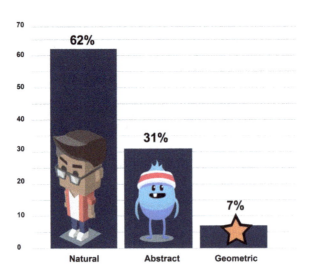

Examples of natural, abstract and geometric forms indicating their percentage distribution in the newsgames studied.

The colors used to represent the games were dominated by bright color palettes (28 games or 56% of the data set). These games used colors with high hue and or brightness. The next largest group, at 26% or 13 games, used dark palettes. Another 9 games, or 18%, had neutral color palettes.

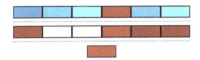

Bright Color Palette: EpiPen Tycoon

Dark Color Palette: The
Amazon Race

Neutral Color Palette: The Ocean Game

Observations and Findings

Confirming the definition of newsgame most commonly emphasized by Frasca, Mateas, Treanor nearly half of the games found and studied were editorial games. This may be an indication of some of the expected rhetorical propensities of the medium, but could also be an indication of selection bias, audience response (e.g. editorial games are perhaps more popular), or a myriad of other observations beyond the scope of an analysis of 50 games. Suffice it to say that editorial newsgames and toys are a continued practice more than 10 years after Frasca had first articulated their possibility. The nearly 25 examples in this set came not only from independent designers and small game companies, but also from major news organizations. This is perhaps the most important finding – that the practice of creating editorial newsgames has been adopted by major news sources. This is in sharp contrast to the foundational work which was largely created by individual artists, academic researchers and their game making companies.

It is also likely unsurprising that the most common mechanic in the set were choose your own adventure games. Such games are relatively easy to author in the conventional software environment and skillsets in news organizations. Thanks to tools like Twine, which the team behind Commuter Challenge(https://wamu.org/commuter-challenge/), used, production costs and technical requirements are rather low. The mechanics is also a narrative form with a long and relatively familiar history, which fits well into the storytelling orientation of some news orgs. What's interesting to note is that choose your own adventure mechanics were not the clear mechanic of choice by much of the seminal newsgame work. Instead, version of action games were more common.

That action is the second most common mechanics is likewise unsurprising, as the action games catalogued are typically translations of action mechanics common to games as early as the 1980's. Beyond the obvious precedent set by the first generation of newsgame and toy creators, there are likely some practical reasons for this. If design teams need to communicate their plans to make a newsgame or toy to editors, both choose your own adventure and action mechanics are commonly understood and full of decades of examples. American Mall Game (https://www.bloomberg.com/features/american-mall-game/) is a good example of an amalgam of action mechanics with plenty of historical reference. Of course, what's most interesting to the community of designers are the novel experiences based on relatively unprecedented mechanics, of which none from the date represented. This could be an indication of a relatively conservative design practice or that such work did not fall in the subset of 50 games studied.

What this snapshot indicates is that while news games and toys are continuing to be built their innovations remain quite limited. The games take mechanics that have been proven engaging over their more than 40-year history and apply them to news topics. This is not necessarily negative as such design also supports a wider ludo-literacy than new mechanics with which players might struggle. It is perhaps an indication of needing to make sure that the designs are not too complicated. Or more likely, just as an article in the USA is often written toward an 8th grade reading level, these games may be designed toward a similar ludo-literacy. Likewise, designers are likely keeping the technographic and psychographic expectations relatively low to assure a wider possible audience.

Many of the designs assumptions about making useful newsgames are affirmed by the experiential characteristics noted. The games are quick to complete (nearly all under 10 minutes). This is likely a decision related to budget, social media share-ability, and meeting the needs of a satisficing audience. The general split in audio uses in these experiences is also a likely a product of technographics and budget. Where it might be strange to find a collection of educational games with only half of the games using audio at all, the small budgets and limited technological expectations may have driven some designers to ignore audio design entirely. It may also be that some platforms used to implement the games, like Twine or basic HTML5, complicate audio usage or that designers considered that some of the games might be played in serious environments (e.g. at work) where players might not want to be surprised by audio.

Surprisingly, the bright color pallets don't necessarily match the often-dark topics the games cover. This is one of the more surprising findings. The easiest explanation for this is that many editorial games, for example, use bright pallets to create a retro-arcade aesthetic that lampoons the seriousness of the topic. Toys like Thoughts and Prayers (https://www.thoughtsandprayersthegame.com/), for example, focus on gun deaths in the US but employ high contrast reds and yellows (instead of the blacks and grays that might normally be associated with the topic). This aesthetic choice is common to much of the work of Everyday Arcade, which uses pixilation and 8-bit audio to match the characteristics of late 1980's and earl 1990's games. It is unclear if the benefit of such decisions is historically referential (aka a classic arcade look) or favored by generation experience (e.g. the designers are of an age when that particular aesthetic was part of childhood), or something else. More interestingly, it may be that just as the political comic has a distinct black and white pen style, newsgames may be developing an aesthetic style that is derived from the low production costs of pixilation and narrow color pallets.

It is from these observations that a kind of convention of aesthetic and experiential attributes for newsgames can be derived. If a political cartoon is defined by its artistic style, satirical content, and a tendency toward hyperbole, it is evident that newsgames and toys are forming their own general characteristics. From our analysis, newsgames tend to be short experiences (i.e. less than 5 minutes) dominated by some rhetorical message (i.e. editorial in nature). The practice seems to have two dominant mechanics, choose your own adventure narratives that impart the myriad of challenging choices in a news item or as arcade games that critique a contemporary news item. The former has a wider set of aesthetic qualities, using either photographs or rendered art to impart it's narrative. The latter, action-oriented play, tends to employ the simple visual and acoustic aesthetics qualities of 8-bit computer games. These observations may prove useful to designers looking to abide by the successful conventions of prior work or for those who want to break out of convention.

Research Limitations

Obviously a more substantive research analysis would have involved more coders and applied intercoder reliability ratings, as has been done in previous work by the authors. A wider collection of games might also prove useful.

For this work the primary aim was to better support he community of newsgame and news toy makers by providing a snapshot of the characteristics of such experiences. As is often the challenge with such work, there is always a balance between research time and the ever-shifting landscape of its subject. Between the initial draft of this paper and the completion of data collection one prominent newsgame company changed it its name, while other examples have since closed their website. For this reason, the researchers wanted to archive these findings in publication form and through the website as quickly as possible. By analogy, this work is less of a rigorous examination of subject and more of a snapshot of the current state.

List of Newsgames, toys and interactives

Project Title URL	Release Year
Madrid *http://www.newsgaming.com/games/madrid/*	2004
Hothead Zindane: *https://www.corriere.it/Primo_Piano/Sport/2006/07_Luglio/10/pop_zidane.shtml*	2006
Food Import Folly: *http://persuasivegames.com/files/food-import-folly/*	2007
Super Obama World: *https://superobamaworld.com/*	2008
Faith Fighter: *https://molleindustria.org/en/faith-fighter/*	2009
Cutthroat Capitalism: The Game: *https://www.wired.com/2009/07/cutthroat-capitalism-the-game/*	2009
Arizona Justice: *http://lgrace.com/Arizona/index_game.html*	2010
Faith Fighter 2: *https://molleindustria.org/en/faith-fighter-2/index.html*	2012

The ReDistricting Game:
http://www.redistrictinggame.org/game.php

2015

Syrian Journey: Pick Your Own Escape Route:
https://www.bbc.com/news/world-middle-east-32057601

2015

7 Ways to Defy Death:
https://www.washingtonpost.com/graphics/health/defy-death/

2015

Delivery Drone
https://lgrace.com/deliverydrone/

2015

Chair the Fed:
https://www.sffed-education.org/chairthefed/

2016

Good Guy With A Gun:
https://everydayarcade.com/games/good-guy-with-a-gun

2016

Kentucky Derby Quiz: Traditions:
https://www.courier-journal.com/pages/interactives/news-quiz/#4

2016

Science Kombat:
https://www.gameflare.com/online-game/science-kombat/

2016

Bomb The Right Place:
https://everydayarcade.com/games/bomb-the-right-place

2016

Trump Toss:
http://www.thegoparcade.com/game/trump-toss

2016

North Exposure:
https://www.theglobeandmail.com/arts/books-and-media/choose-your-own-profile-ryan-north/article30328294/

2016

Thoughts & Prayers: The Game:
https://everydayarcade.com/games/thoughts-and-prayers-the-game

2016

Get Trump's Taxes:
https://everydayarcade.com/games/get-trumps-taxes

2016

Science Fighter:
https://everydayarcade.com/games/science-fighter

2016

Trumps' Convention Rampage:
https://everydayarcade.com/games/trumps-convention-rampage

2016

Points Of Entry:
http://persuasivegames.com/game/nytimmigration

2016

Windfall:
http://persuasivegames.com/game/windfall

2016

Angry Olds:
https://everydayarcade.com/games/angry-olds

2016

Epipen Tycoon:
https://everydayarcade.com/games/epipen-tycoon

2016

The Voter Suppression Trail:
https://everydayarcade.com/games/the-voter-suppression-trail

2016

Trump's Pussy Grabber:
http://www.thegoparcade.com/game/trumps-pussy-grabber

2016

#Hacked:
https://syhacked.com

2016

Square Off: A Final Fantasy 7- Inspired Trivia Game:
https://www.polygon.com/a/final-fantasy-7/battle-trivia

2017

Commuter Challenge:
https://wamu.org/commuter-challenge/

2017

The Good, The Bad and The Accountant:
https://jplusplus.github.io/the-accountant/#/

2017

Build Your Own Trading Bot:
https://www.wsj.com/graphics/build-your-own-trading-bot/

2017

Payback:
https://www.timeforpayback.com/

2017

The Uber Game:
https://ig.ft.com/uber-game/

2017

College Scholarship Tycoon:
https://www.vox.com/policy-and-politics/2017/11/1/16526202/college-scholarship-tycoon-game

2017

Hurl the Harasser:
http://hurl.persuasiveplay.org/

2017

Brexit Bus:
https://advisa.se/en/research/brexit-bus/

2017

Factitious:
http://factitious.augamestudio.com/#/

2017

American Mall Game:
https://www.bloomberg.com/features/american-mall-game/

2018

You are Jeff Bezos, where would the HQ2 go?
http://gatehousenews.com/amazon

2018

Budget Game of Survival:
*https://graphics.straitstimes.com/STI/STIMEDIA/Intera
ctives/2018/02/game-of-survival-budget-2018/index.html*

2018

Get Bad News:
https://getbadnews.com/#intro

2018

The Waiting Game:
https://projects.propublica.org/asylum/

2018

MTA Country:
https://everydayarcade.com/games/mta-country

2018

Could You Be A Cricket Umpire:
*https://www.thetimes.co.uk/article/cricket-umpire-lbw-game-
tg06rcv7s*

2018

Think Military Strike Could Stop North Korea? Try It And See: *https://www.nytimes.com/interactive/2018/05/24/opinion /north-korea-trump-military-strikes.html*	2018
What Makes a World Cup Winner: *https://www.telegraph.co.uk/world-cup/world-cup-2018- winners-predictions-forecast-champions/*	2018
Dumb Ways To Kill Oceans: *https://gamingfortheoceans.org/*	2018
The Betsy Devos Board Game: *https://www.washingtonpost.com/graphics/2018/lifestyle/m agazine/ben-folds-artists-alternative-storytelling- issue/?noredirect=on#pg-devos*	2018
Two Billion Miles: *http://twobillionmiles.com/*	2018
Dodging Trump's Tariffs: *https://ig.ft.com/trump-china-tariffs/*	2019
The Amazon Race: *https://mobile.abc.net.au/news/2019-02-27/amazon- warehouse-workers-game-race/10803346*	2019
Dumb Ways To Die 2: *http://www.dumbwaystodie.com/dumb-ways-to-die-2-the- games/*	2019
Order! Order! Could You Be Speaker: *https://www.thetimes.co.uk/article/could-you-be-speaker- house-of-commons-bercow-xck6lxv98*	2019

The Ocean Game: The Sea is Rising, Can You Save Your Town?   2019
https://www.latimes.com/projects/la-me-climate-change-ocean-game/

Choose Your Own Adventure: Renting: 2019
https://www.vice.com/en_uk/article/9ke547/choose-your-own-adventure-renting

How Does An Autonomous Car Work? Not So Great: 2019
https://www.washingtonpost.com/graphics/2019/business/how-does-an-autonomous-car-work/

Covid-19 Trivia: 2020
http://professorgrace.com/covid/game.html

Gaming the System: 2020
https://gamingthesystem.journalismgames.com/

ACKNOWLEDGMENTS

The research team would like to acknowledge the John S. and James L. Knight Foundation for continued support in innovations in news and this research.

REFERENCES

[1] Bogost, Ian, Simon Ferrari, and Bobby Schweizer. *Newsgames: Journalism at play.* MIT Press, 2012.

[2] Foxman, Maxwell Henry. "Play the news: Fun and games in digital journalism." (2015). Tow Center for Digital Journalism. https://www.cjr.org/tow_center_reports/play_the_news_fun_and_games_in_digital_journalism.php

[3] Frasca, Gonzalo. "Play the message: Play, game and videogame rhetoric." *Unpublished PhD dissertation. IT University of Copenhagen, Denmark* (2007).

[4] Frasca, Gonzalo. "September 12th". 2003.

[5] Grace, Lindsay, Mike Treanor, Chris Totten, and Josh McCoy. "A Case Study in Newsgame Creation: Why Game Designers and Journalists are Still Learning to Work Together." In *66th International Communication Conference, Fokouka, Japan.* 2016.

[6] Grace, Lindsay D., and Maggie Farley. "How game design thinking becomes engagement design." *Proceedings of the 20th International Academic Mindtrek Conference.* ACM, 2016.

[7] Grace, Lindsay D. *Doing Things with Games: Social Impact Through Play.* CRC Press, 2019.

[8] Meier, Klaus. "Journalism meets games: Newsgames as a new digital genre. Theory, boundaries, utilization." *Journal of Applied Journalism & Media Studies* 7.2 (2018): 429-444.

[9] Ostermann, Ana Cristina, and Deborah Keller-Cohen. "Good girls go to heaven; bad girls...'learn to be good: quizzes in American and Brazilian teenage girls' magazines." *Discourse & Society* 9.4 (1998): 531-558.

[10] Plewe, Christoph, and Elfriede Fürsich. "Are newsgames better journalism? Empathy, information and representation in games on refugees and migrants." *Journalism Studies* 19.16 (2018): 2470-2487.

[11] Ruiz, Susana, Ashley York, Mike Stein, Noah Keating, and Kellee Santiago. "Darfur is dying." *Computer software. mtvU* (2006).

[12] Plewe, Christoph, and Elfriede Fürsich. "Are newsgames better journalism? Empathy, information and representation in games on refugees and migrants." *Journalism Studies* 19.16 (2018): 2470-2487.

[13] Sicart, Miguel. "Newsgames: Theory and design." *International Conference on Entertainment Computing.* Springer, Berlin, Heidelberg, 2008.

[14] Treanor, Mike, and Michael Mateas. "Newsgames-Procedural Rhetoric Meets Political Cartoons." *DiGRA Conference.* 2009.

[15]Siitonen, Marko, Panu Uotila, Turo Uskali, Jukka Varsaluoma, and Tanja Välisalo. "A Pilot Study on Developing Newsgames in Collaboration between Journalism and Computer Science Students." *Nordicom Review* 40, no. 2 (2019).

[16]Vobic, Igor, Lea Dvorsak, and Mojca Vtic. "DIGITAL GAMES AND JOURNALISM: A CASE-STUDY OF SLOVENIAN POLITICAL WEEKLY'S NEWSGAME-MLADINA'S FOJBA 2000." *Teorija in praksa* 51.1 (2014): 123.

www.ingramcontent.com/pod-product-compliance
Lightning Source LLC
Chambersburg PA
CBHW070905070326
40690CB00009B/2007